To _____

From_____

Date _____

Read-Aloud
Stories

Read-Aloud Stories

Samuel J. Butcher, *illustrator*

BAKER BOOK HOUSE
Grand Rapids, Michigan 49516

Library of Congress Cataloging-in-Publication Data

Precious moments : read-aloud stories / edited by Debbie Butcher
    Wiersma / illustrations by Samuel J. Butcher.
          p.   cm.
    Summary: Brief story-poems focus on such areas as "My
Family," "Playtime," and "Feelings." sometimes highlighting
God's role in our lives.
    ISBN 0-8010-1015-2
    [1. Christian life—Fiction. w. Stories in rhyme.] I. Wiersma,
Debbie Butcher. II. Butcher, Samuel J. (Samuel John), 1939–
ill.
PZ8.3.P8893   1992
[E]—dc20   91-27064

Contents

Animal Friends

Silly Words

I wonder why
A hen would
    CLUCK.
Wouldn't you think
A DUCK would
    CLUCK?

And why do you think
A mouse would SQUEAK?
Maybe he didn't get
OILED this week!

Sam B

Some animals talk
In the silliest way.
It makes me giggle to hear them say:
CLUCK, CLUCK, HEE-HAW,
COCK-A-DOODLE-DOO!
I think that's funny,
How about you?

Why would a rooster
Like to CROW?
I would think
A CROW would CROW!

And when an owl
Says, "WHOO are you?"
Should I say,
"I'm ME, that's WHO?"

Animal Friends

Some animals talk
In the funniest way.
I have to laugh
When I hear them say
CLUCK! CLUCK! HEE-HAW!
COCK-A-DOODLE-DO!
They make me happy,
How about you?

Who Sleeps Where?

Would a big huge elephant
Sleep inside a tiny tent?
  No-o-o.
Elephants sleep
  in the jungle.

Does a little baby deer
Sleep inside a giant's ear?
 No-o-o.
A deer sleeps
 in the tall grass.

Would a blue bird in the night
Sleep atop a flying kite?
 No-o-o.
Blue birds sleep
 in their warm nests.

Does a little cubby bear
Sleep beneath a rocking chair?
 No-o-o.
Bear cubs sleep
 in a quiet cave.

Does a baby kangaroo
Sleep inside his daddy's shoe?
  No-o-o.
A baby kangaroo
  sleeps in his mother's pouch.

And would a little girl or boy
Sleep inside their favorite toy?
   No-o-o.
Little boys and girls sleep
   in a nice, warm bed
with a soft and gentle kiss
   on each one's little head.

Pretty Kitty

Kitty, kitty,
Pretty kitty.
Where were you born?
In the Big, Big City?
Was there a town
Where you lived at?
Or was your mom
a country cat?
Where did you come from,
little one?
A far-off land
behind the sun?
My newest friend
so soft and pretty,
I sure love you,
my Birthday Kitty.

Pets in
Backward Land

In Backward Land
there lives a cat
Who can't ME-OW
this way or that.
For when she tries
ME-OW, you see,
This Backward Cat
will say OW-ME.

In Backward Land
   there lives a cow
Who wants to MOO
   as cows know how.
But when she tries
   to MOO her way,
OOOOM is all
   this cow can say.

And in that Land
   that's all mixed up
There lives a
   very little pup.
But when he tries
   to bark his way,
WOW BOW is all
   this dog can say.

In Backward Land
   you don't keep pets,
But pets keep you
   on their front steps.
I know you're glad
   that you can stay
Where God made things
   a better way.

The Lonely Frog

There was once a lonely frog who lived alone near a quiet pond. He was lonely because he was the only frog who lived there. Mr. Frog wanted to marry a beautiful girl frog. But he was sure that no beautiful girl frog would like him. Of course, he had never seen a girl frog. So he wasn't even sure what one looked like.

One day, an owl flew onto a limb over the pond. The lonely frog began to tell the owl his troubles.

"I want to marry a beautiful girl frog," he said. "But I have this terrible habit. You have never seen anyone with such a terrible habit."

"Whoooo?" asked the owl.

"Me," said the lonely frog.

"I am ashamed of the way I eat," Mr. Frog said. "Watch this!"

The frog flipped out his long tongue and zapped a fly going by.

"See?" said the lonely frog. "No beautiful girl frog would want to marry someone who eats like that."

Mr. Owl nodded. "I see what you mean," he said in a wise old voice. "I certainly

wouldn't want to marry someone who eats like that."

Mr. Frog hung his head. "What will I do?" he asked.

Mr. Owl thought for a moment. "Come with me," he said. "But be very quiet."

The owl led the lonely frog to another pond. It really wasn't that far, but the lonely frog had never been there. He did not even know there was another pond. "Shhh," said the owl. "Stay behind this tree and watch."

Suddenly Mr. Frog saw a girl frog. He thought she was the most beautiful girl frog in the whole world. His heart went pitter-patter.

"Shh," said the owl, as the girl frog came out on the lily pad to eat dinner. "Watch."

The lonely frog was embarrassed to watch her eat dinner. But he did what the owl said.

Suddenly a fly buzzed in front of the girl
frog. ZAPPPP! Out went her long tongue
and zapped the fly. Her tongue was almost
as long as the lonely frog's tongue!

Mr. Frog was so excited that he jumped up and down, even more than frogs usually do. "She eats just like me," he shouted. He shouted so loud that the girl frog saw him there.

"Just as I thought," said the owl. "All frogs eat like that. And a habit can't be terrible if that's the way God made you!"

Now the lonely frog wasn't lonely any more. The beautiful girl frog thought he was the most handsome boy frog she had ever seen, and they soon had a wonderful lily pad wedding.

My Family

I Can't Wait

"I can't wait," said Allen. He licked his lips as he watched his mom mix the cookie dough.

She smiled and said, "Be patient, Allen. The cookies will taste much better than this dough. Anyway, it's too close to dinnertime. But you may have two cookies after dinner."

Mom put little balls of dough on a cookie sheet and popped them in the oven.

"I can't wait," Allen said again. He watched each thing his mother did.

"After dinner," said Mom.

Before long, wonderful smells went through the house. Allen tried not to think about the cookies. But how could he help it with those wonderful smells?

"I just can't wait," Allen said to his mother.

"I know," said Mom. "It's hard to wait, but there are two cookies for you after dinner."

Later his mother took the cookies from the oven. They were very hot.

"Mmmmm," said Allen. "Could I have one of my two cookies now?"

"They are much too hot to eat," Mom said. "But I promised you two cookies after dinner. Okay?"

"But I can't wait," Allen moaned.

His mother smiled. "Yes, you can," she said. "Just be patient."

 **My Family**

Allen ran outside to play. Perhaps he would not smell the cookies out there. But he *thought* about the cookies out there. And he *kept* thinking about the cookies. Every time he tried to think about playing, he would think how good those cookies would taste.

"I can't wait," said Allen. "But Mom says I have to until after dinner."

Before long, Allen ran into the house. Now he smelled the cookies again. The wonderful smell was everywhere in the house.

Allen watched Mom put the cookies in the cookie jar. He watched her put the cookie jar on the shelf.

"Dinner will be ready in a few minutes," she said. "After dinner you may have two cookies."

"But I can't wait," said Allen.

His mother smiled. She was sure she had heard Allen say that before.

"I have some work that I have to finish. When I'm ready, we will eat dinner," said Mom. "I'll be in my room for a few minutes."

When his mother left the room, Allen looked at the cookie jar. He looked at a stool near the cookie-jar shelf.

"I can't wait," Allen said to himself. "I really can't wait."

Allen put the stool by the shelf. He stood on the stool and reached for the cookie jar. But he felt bad as soon as he touched the cookie jar. He knew he should not do this.

Allen started to get down from the stool. Suddenly he smelled the cookies again.

"No one will miss just one cookie," he whispered to himself.

Allen stood on the stool again. He reached up. This time he picked up the

cookie jar. He was sure his mother would never know.

Suddenly Mom called from the other room. "I'm almost finished," she said. "Then we'll have dinner."

As soon as Allen heard his mother's voice, he started to put the cookie jar back on the shelf. But something terrible happened. The jar slipped from his hands. It fell to the floor with a crash!

Allen looked at the cookie jar.

Mom came running and then *she* looked at the cookie jar.

Allen looked at Mom.

Mom looked at Allen.

"Look at all that broken glass mixed with those cookies," said his mother. "We will have to throw all of them away."

A tear came from Allen's eye. "I'm sorry, Mom," he said. "I shouldn't have done that. Now I really will have to wait."

"Yes, you will," his mother said with a sad smile. "I won't have time to make more cookies for quite a while."

When he went to bed that night, Allen was sure he could still smell the cookies.

"Maybe we'll make some more cookies next weekend," Mom said as she tucked him in.

Allen started to say, "I can't wait." But he didn't.

"I CAN wait," he said. "Next time I'll wait until you say I can have a cookie."

Allen closed his eyes and prayed. "Thank you, God," he said. "Thank you for helping me to learn to wait even when I don't want to."

A Secret Special Someone

A secret special
someone
Has washed
and ironed
my clothes.

I think I'll hide and find her,
Or ask someone who knows.
    I wonder who this special person is?

A secret special someone
Has made my bed today.
Now who would do a thing like that
When I ran out to play?
    I wonder who this special person is?

A secret special someone
Cleaned up my toys for me.
I must find out who did it,
I think I'll wait and see.
  I wonder who this special person is?

A secret special someone
is cooking dinner, too.
I caught you, Special Someone,
Why, Mommy Dear! It's YOU!

44

Mother's Cookies

Today I was playing in the living room. Suddenly I smelled something wonderful. It was coming from the kitchen, so guess where I ran!

Mommy smiled at me.

"Smell something good?" she asked.

"I smell something *very* good," I answered. "Are you baking cookies?"

"Do they smell like cookies?" she asked.

I nodded my head.

"You can smell many wonderful things," Mommy said. "You can smell cookies baking or hot pancakes on a winter morning. You can smell flowers or new shoes. You can smell fresh bread at home or popcorn at the zoo."

I don't think about smelling very much. But Mommy's cookies helped me remember what a wonderful gift God gave me.

"Thank you, God, for a nose to smell good things with," I prayed.

Before long Mommy took the cookies from the oven. They were beautiful. She had cut many different shapes. There were animals and stars and hearts and circles. Mommy sprinkled decorations on the cookies to make them red and green and orange and silver. Some cookies were very big and some were little.

"Do these look like cookies?" Mommy asked.

I nodded my head.

"You can see many wonderful things," Mommy said. "You can see cookies and cats and dogs and trees. You can see lions and tigers and monkeys at the zoo. You can see your birthday gifts when you open them."

I don't think about seeing very much but Mommy's cookies helped me remember what a wonderful gift God gave me.

"Thank you, God, for two eyes to see good things with," I prayed.

By this time the cookies were cool enough to eat. "Time to test a cookie," said Mommy. "You can have the first one."

I picked up a cookie. It was soft and warm.

"Do you feel that soft, warm cookie?" Mommy asked. "You can feel many wonderful things. You can feel soft, warm cookies and cuddly teddy bears. You can feel the hot rays of a summer sun. You can feel cold ice cream and ice cubes and the cold winter wind on your cheeks outside. You can feel a hard ball and your woolly sweater. And you can feel my hugs and my kiss on your cheek."

I don't think about feeling things very much. But Mommy's soft, warm cookie in my hand helped me remember what a wonderful gift God gave me.

"Thank you, God, for two hands to feel things with," I prayed.

"Time to take a bite," said Mommy.

Her cookie was so good. I was sure that one would never be enough. Mommy

thought so, too. She said I could have another one.

"Do you taste the flavor of your cookie?" Mommy asked. "You can taste warm sugar cookies and hot chocolate. You can taste strawberries and oranges and grapes. You can taste a sweet lollipop and a sour pickle. God helps you taste many, many things."

I don't think about tasting very much — but Mommy's yummy cookie helped me remember what a wonderful gift God gave me.

"Thank you, God, for giving me a mouth to taste good things with," I prayed.

"Can you hear cookies?" Mommy asked.

I laughed. "I can hear you," I said. "I hear you telling me lots of special things about your cookies."

"You can hear many other wonderful things, too," said Mommy. "You can hear

your puppy bark and your kitty purr. You can hear music and friends laughing. And you can hear the wind sighing in the trees. God helps you hear many things."

I almost never think about hearing, but hearing Mommy's voice telling me about these things helped me remember what a wonderful gift God gave me.

"Thank you, God, for giving me ears to hear so many sounds," I prayed.

"Did you like my cookies?" Mommy asked.

"I like to smell your cookies, see your cookies, feel your cookies, and taste your cookies," I said. "And I like to hear all the special things your cookies taught me."

Mommy smiled.

"Thank you, God, for sweet cookies," I prayed. "And oh, yes, thank you especially for my own sweet Mommy."

Playtime

A Box with Blocks and Clocks

I have one box.
Will you play with me
   inside my box?

I have two blocks.

Will you play
   with my blocks
   inside my box?

I have three tick-tock clocks.

Will you play
   with my blocks
   inside my box
   with the tick-tock clocks?

I have four rocks.

Will you play
 with my rocks
 inside my box
 with the blocks
 and the tick-tock clocks?

You have five smelly socks?
 Please don't
 play with me
 in my box!

57

Playtime Can Be Fun

"Playing with Annie is not fun," said Arnie. "When I want to play with marbles she wants to play make-believe. When I want to play with trucks and cars, she wants to have a tea party."

Mom smiled. She had heard that before.

"Playing with Arnie is no fun either," said Annie. "When I want to play 'house,' he wants to play football. When I want to play 'school,' he wants to fly his airplane."

Mom smiled again. She had also heard that before.

"Why can't Annie be more fun?" asked Arnie.

"Why can't Arnie be more fun?" asked Annie.

"Do you really want Annie to be more fun?" Mom asked Arnie.

"Yes, I really do," said Arnie.

"Do you really want Arnie to be more fun?" Mom asked Annie.

"Sure, I do," said Annie.

"Arnie, if you want Annie to be more fun, you must pull together more with her in playtime," said Mom. "And Annie, if you want Arnie to be more fun, you must pull together more with him in playtime."

Annie and Arnie both looked puzzled.

"Pull together?" asked Annie.

"How do we do that?" asked Arnie.

Mom pulled a book off of the children's shelf.

"Let's look for some pictures," she said. "Maybe they will help you understand."

"Here's one," said Mom. She held up a picture of two horses pulling a wagon. "What are the two horses doing?"

"They're pulling a wagon," said Arnie.

"They're also pulling together," said Mom. "But let's pretend. What if one horse was hitched to the front of the wagon and one was hitched to the back of the wagon. Each pulls in the opposite direction."

Annie and Arnie laughed. "They might pull the wagon apart," said Annie.

"And they sure wouldn't go very far or very fast," said Arnie.

"So which is better for the horses, to pull together or to pull apart?" asked Mom.

"Pull together," said Arnie. Annie nodded her head yes.

"Oh, look," said Mom. "Here's another picture. What are this boy and this girl doing?"

"Riding a bike," said Annie.

"They're also riding it together," said Mom. "They're riding in the same direction. But let's pretend. What if the boy tries to

pedal in one direction and the girl tries to pedal in the other direction?"

"They wouldn't get very far," said Arnie.

"And they wouldn't have much fun," said Annie.

"Pulling together IS more fun," said Mom.

"Yes," said Annie. "But how can Arnie and I pull together as we play?"

"Yeah," said Arnie. "How do we do that?"

"Arnie, why don't you like to play the games that Annie enjoys?" asked Mom.

"I just don't like them," said Arnie. "I'm too old to play those games."

"Annie, why didn't you want to play with Arnie's football and trucks, marbles and airplanes?" asked Mother.

"Because I like my games better," said Annie.

"So Arnie wants to play with his toys and Annie wants to play with her toys," said

Mom. "Is that pulling together or pulling apart?"

Arnie and Annie knew the answer to that.

"That's fine if you want to play alone," Mom said. "But maybe it would be more fun to play with things that you both enjoy so that you can play together."

"Things like what?" asked Annie.

"Well, you tell me," Mom said. "Let's see how many toys and games you can name that you both like."

In less than three minutes Annie and Arnie had named three games, four toys, and five books they both liked. And before you could say "pull together" they were having fun together with one of the games.

"Pulling together," Mom smiled as she left the room. "That's what playtime should be."

Ellie's Elephant

"They're so funny," said Ellie.

Ellie and Dad had laughed as they watched the elephants at the zoo. Ellie thought they were about the funniest elephants she had ever seen.

"Look at that," said Ellie. "The elephant is feeding herself with her nose."

"Actually it's called a trunk," said Dad. "But it is like a nose, isn't it?"

"And she can squirt water and make her own shower," said Ellie. "I wish I had that elephant for a pet."

Dad laughed. "What would you do with your new pet?" he asked.

"I'd dress her up in something pretty," said Ellie. "Maybe we'd pretend we were clowns in a circus. We'd have so much fun together!"

Then Ellie thought how hard it would be to dress and undress her elephant. It would be a big job!

"That's not such a good idea after all," said Ellie. "I will think of something else for my elephant pet to do."

"I know," she said. "We could play in my little pool in the backyard." Ellie thought of her elephant and the little plastic pool. But if Ellie's elephant sat in the pool she would squash it flat like a pancake. Then all the

water would run out into the yard. Of course the pool would be broken and have to be thrown away.

"That's not such a good idea either," said Ellie. "Let me think of something else."

Then she had another idea. "My pet elephant can take me to school each day," she said. "I won't have to ride the school bus any more."

Ellie thought about her fast school bus. Elephants usually walk very slowly. She could be late. What if her pet elephant wouldn't go any faster? Ellie's teacher would make her stay after school. She might even make Ellie's pet elephant stay after school, too. But her pet elephant would probably knock over the tables and desks and books.

Ellie's Elephant

"No, no, no!" said Ellie. "That's not a good idea. I must think of something else for my pet elephant to do."

Ellie thought about keeping her pet elephant in her room. But she knew that would not be a good idea. She even thought about her pet elephant rinsing the dinner dishes, but she was sure her mother wouldn't like that idea, either.

"Maybe when you and Mom want me to water the flowers in the yard, my pet elephant could do it for me," Ellie said. Then

71

she thought that the water might come from her elephant's trunk too fast, and that would hurt the flowers instead of helping them. Ellie's elephant might step on the flowers, too. No, that would not be a good idea.

Ellie thought about her pet elephant awhile. Then she began to smile.

"I have the best idea of all," said Ellie.

Now Dad smiled. "I'm sure it must be very good," he said.

"Oh, it is!" said Ellie. "I think my pet elephant should stay here in the zoo. She can do what elephants do best and have her own elephant friends. And I can come often to visit her."

"That really **is** the best idea of all," said Dad.

Make-Believe

Candyland

The other day
   at the Licorice Log,
I had a talk
   with the Gumdrop Dog.
I asked him, "What's
   that under your hat?"
And he said, "It's just
   the Chocolate Cat."
I asked him why
   the Cat was there,
He said, "It's combing
   my Caramel Hair."

Make-Believe

But the Marshmallow Mouse
   came scampering past.
Which made that Cat
   run very fast.
It raced that Mouse
   down Lemon Drop Lane.
They laughed as they raced
   to the Candy Cane.
The Chocolate Cat
   made friends
   with the Mouse,
Now they live together
   in the Gingerbread House.

Friends in
Backward Land

In Backward Land
  a boy is there
Who wears his shoes
  up in his hair.
Each morning he
  must comb his toes,
And look behind him
  with his nose.

Make-Believe

A girl is there
    in Backward Land,
Who has five toes
    upon each hand.
When she says "thanks,"
    it sounds like "please."
And when she's hot,
    this girl will freeze.

Another boy
    who's very nice
Goes swimming in
    a lake of ice.
And on the brightest
    sunny day,
He wears his raincoat
    out to play.

One girl's toothbrush
   filled with paste
Scrubs all the teeth
   around her waist.
She holds her hair
   to stop her sneeze,
And then this girl
   will comb her knees.

If you lived there
   in Backward Land,
You might wear boots
   upon your hand.
You'd wear your gloves
   upon your toes.
And pull your socks
   up to your nose.

I know you're glad
   that you live here,
Where you can listen
   with your ear.
Where socks are worn
   upon your feet.
And all you do
   is really neat.

I know you're glad
   that God made you
To do the things
   you like to do,
To be the you
   that's truly you.
And live the way
   He wants you to.

Do You Know?

Do You
See Me, God?

Dear God,
You are so big.
You made me so small.
Sometimes I wonder if You
   really see me.
I see the stars.
I see the moon.
I know You made them
   with Your hands.
You must see me.

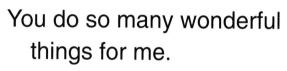

You do so many wonderful
   things for me.
I want to do something for
   You.
I will help You
   take care
of Your beautiful
   world.
Thank You, God.
You're wonderful!

From Psalm 8:3–9

What Am I?

I am not a square, circle, or triangle.
Nothing else is shaped exactly like me.
What am I?

I am hard on the
outside, but soft
and gooey on the
inside.

What am I?

If you break me I am broken forever. You can never glue me back together again.

What am I?

If you keep me warm, you may get a baby bird,
chicken,
turkey,
duck,
goose,
or even
a snake
from me.

That's because I came
from one of these things.

Do you know who I am yet?

Now you know, don't you?

Workers

Delivery Boy

Rick was excited. "I'm going to earn some money," he told his mother. "I'm going to get rich."

"Really?" Mother asked. "How do you plan to get rich?"

"Delivering groceries at Sam's Supermarket," said Rick. "There's an ad in the paper for a delivery boy."

Mother smiled as Rick waved good-bye. "Don't you want your red wagon?" she asked.

"Nope. Who needs an old wagon?" said Rick. "I'm big. I can do anything."

Rick waved good-bye and ran all the way to Sam's Supermarket.

"You're the first boy here," said Sam. "Good. I have two bags of groceries for Mrs. Collins. I'll give you a quarter a bag to deliver. But don't you have a wagon?"

"Nope, who needs an old wagon?" said Rick. "I'm big. I can do anything."

"Do it your way," said Sam. "Just get the groceries there. Okay?"

"Okay," said Rick.

Rick picked up one bag of groceries in each arm. Sam watched as Rick huffed and puffed all the way to the door. But Rick couldn't open the door. He had a bag of groceries in each arm.

Rick put one bag down while he opened the door. He grunted and groaned when he had to pick it back up again.

"I still think a wagon would help," Sam said.

"I'm big. I can do anything," said Rick.

"Okay, you may be big and maybe you can do anything," said Sam. "But I think you've still got a lot to learn."

Rick started down the street, huffing and puffing with the two bags. Suddenly he felt something wet. Rick looked at the grocery bags. The frozen things were melting and the bottom of one bag was wet.

Rick could see that he'd never be able to carry both bags all the way to Mrs. Collins's house. So he walked back to Sam's.

Rick set the dry bag down. "I'll make two trips," he told Sam. "I need the exercise anyway."

"Sure," said Sam. "Just get the groceries there. OK?"

Rick picked up the wet bag and started down the street. Sam watched him as he went. "He's got a few things to learn," Sam mumbled.

Suddenly the bottom of the wet bag burst open. All of the groceries fell to the sidewalk.

Rick ran back to Sam's. "I . . . I think you gave me a wet bag," Rick said. "I'll put all of this stuff in a dry bag and take it right over."

"I gave you a wet bag?" asked Sam. "Maybe you should look where you put the other bag."

Rick looked at the second bag. He had put it on some wet spots on the floor. Now

he was really in trouble because the second bag was wet too.

"Looks like I need two dry bags," said Rick. "I also need my red wagon."

By the time Rick packed all the groceries into dry bags, he was tired. But he ran all the way home for his red wagon. Then he pulled both bags in his wagon to Mrs. Collins's house.

"Are you rich yet?" Mother asked when Rick came home.

Rick smiled. "I didn't make lots of money," he said. "But I learned three very important lessons today."

Do you know the three important lessons Rick learned?

He learned that:

1. Even though you think you're big, you may still need help with things.

2. It's not right to try to blame your mistakes on someone else.

3. It's okay to admit when you're wrong.

Jake the Baker

Jake the baker
Baked a cake.
The cake
Jake baked
Began to shake.

100

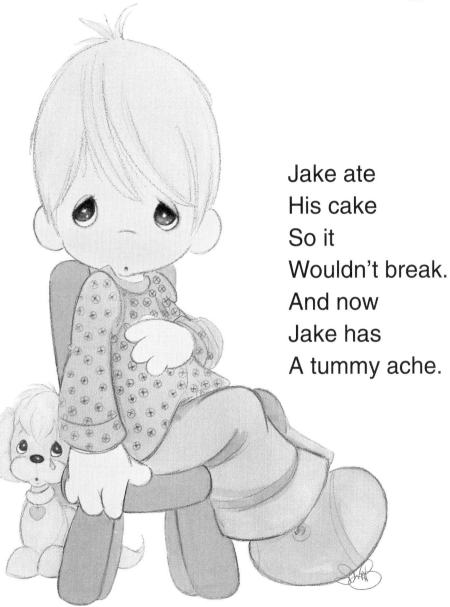

Jake ate
His cake
So it
Wouldn't break.
And now
Jake has
A tummy ache.

The Auctioneer

Mitch had never been to an auction before. He had never seen an auctioneer. And he had never heard a man talk as fast as the auctioneer did at this auction.

"What do I hear for this wonderful pitcher?" the man asked. "$10.00, going once, going twice, gone! Sold to the lady in blue for $10.00!"

"Why does he talk so fast?" Mitch asked Mother.

"He wants to get people excited about the things he is selling," said Mother. "If people get excited about something, they may buy it."

"Is it an auctioneer's job to get people excited about buying?" asked Mitch.

"What do you mean?" asked Mother.

"Well, you always get me excited about Christmas and birthday gifts," said Mitch. "But, you don't get me excited about buying them. You get me excited about getting them as gifts. And you don't talk that fast. So I wondered if it's only the auctioneer's job to get people excited about buying. Or are you an auctioneer, too?"

"An auctioneer for gifts," said Mother. "What an interesting idea. Do you think I could be an auctioneer for your birthday or Christmas gifts? Is that the way I should get you excited about receiving them?"

Mitch laughed. He tried to think of Mother talking fast like an auctioneer.

"Are you an auctioneer?" asked Mitch.

"I suppose I am," said Mother. "I do get you excited about receiving your gifts. But I don't do it the way this auctioneer does."

"Is God an auctioneer, too?" asked Mitch. "Does he get us excited about receiving the gifts he gives us?"

"Well," said Mother, "He does get us excited about his wonderful gifts to us."

Mitch thought about the auctioneer. He thought about God's gifts to him. He smiled.

"I can hear him now," said Mitch. "What do I hear for this wonderful ray of sunshine? Going once. Going twice. Sold to Mother. But it won't cost you a penny."

"That was good, Mitch," said Mother. "Now let me try one. What do I hear for this beautiful sunset? Going once. Going twice. Sold to Mitch. But it won't cost you a penny either."

Mitch and Mother laughed. They thought of God auctioning the rain, a field of wildflowers, a million trees in autumn, ten thousand beautiful birds flying across the sky, white puffy clouds, and lots of other great gifts. But, of course, not one of them cost Mitch or Mother a penny.

"God does give us some wonderful gifts," said Mitch. "And we should get excited about them!"

On the way home, Mitch and Mother made a long list of God's special gifts. And they were excited about each one.

Things to Think About

Do Angels Fly?

"That was a good Christmas play tonight," Dad said. "You were a good angel, Rhonda. And you were a good shepherd, Rod."

"That was fun," said Rhonda. "I wish I could really be an angel."

Dad smiled. "Usually you are like a little angel," he said. "Is that good enough?"

"I've never seen an angel," Rod said. "Have you, Dad?"

"No, I've never seen a real angel," his Father said. "But the Bible has many stories about angels. Your Christmas play tonight was only one story."

"Do angels really fly?" asked Rhonda.

"Do they have wings?" asked Rod. "Or do they fly in airplanes?"

"The Bible doesn't say if they have wings," Dad answered. "Some angel-like creatures called cherubim had wings. Perhaps angels did, too. But they did go places in a hurry. And they were sometimes in the sky. Sometimes they came from heaven. Perhaps they do have wings. Somehow they can appear where they want to be."

"Wow, I would love to see a real angel," said Rod.

"But what do angels do?" asked Rhonda. "Do they help us?"

"God sent angels with special messages," said Dad. "In your play, an angel brought the shepherds a special message about Jesus."

"Is that all they do?" asked Rod.

"Sometimes angels protect or help God's people," Dad said.

"So I can do any dangerous thing I want, and the angels will take care of me?" Rod asked.

"No, you can't," said Dad.

"Why not?" asked Rhonda.

"God knows what is best for each of us," Dad answered. "We must trust him to protect us at the right time. But we have to take care of ourselves, too."

"Are angels here with us right now?" Rod asked.

"Perhaps," said Father.

"I'm glad God sends angels to help us and give us good news," said Rhonda.

"Me, too," said Rod.

Father gave his children a big hug. "And I'm glad that God sent my two little angels to me," he said with a smile.

A Shepherd Song

What does a shepherd
   feed his lamb?
Good green grass
   or gooseberry jam?

What does a shepherd
   tell his sheep?
"Stay up all night,"
   or "Go to sleep"?

What does a shepherd
    like to say?
"Find it yourself," or
    "I'll show you the way"?

What does a shepherd
    like to do?
He likes to whisper,
    "I love you."

The Best Gift of All

"How was Sunday school this morning?" Mother asked.

"Okay, I guess," said Jason.

"You guess?" Mother asked. "Why do you guess?"

"Our teacher says we should give our best to Jesus," said Jason. "But what does Jesus want? What does he need? What is my best?"

Mother smiled. "What do you think?" she asked.

"I give him some pennies and nickels and dimes in the offering," said Jason. "But I don't think that's my best. I think I need to grow up and make millions of dollars. Then I could give him lots of money."

"A lot of people can give money," said Mother. "Jesus wants you to give money to help with his work. But you asked how you can give YOUR best. What can you give that no one else can give?"

"I could give Jesus my best toys," said Jason. "But I don't think Jesus needs my toys. Doesn't he have other things to play with?"

"Sometimes you can give toys to needy children," said Mother. "Jesus is glad when you do that. A lot of people can give toys. But I don't think that that's YOUR best. What can you give that no one else can give?"

Jason looked puzzled. "I don't know," he said. "I suppose I could give my teddy bear to Jesus. That's one of my favorite things. But how do I do that? And what does Jesus want to do with my teddy bear? He doesn't really need a teddy bear, does he?"

"You could give a teddy bear to another child," said Mother. "Jesus is glad when you do that. But a lot of other people can give their favorite bears, too. So, I don't think that that's YOUR best. What can you give that no one else can give?"

"I guess my very best of all is my kitty or puppy," said Jason. "But Jesus doesn't need a kitty or puppy, does he? And does he really want MY kitty or puppy?"

"I think Jesus wants you to take care of your kitty and puppy for him," said Mother. "That's why you have them. But that really isn't your best. You asked how you can

give YOUR best. What can you give that no one else can give?"

Jason really looked puzzled now. "I don't know," he said. "I guess all that's left is just me."

"And, do you know what, Jason?" Mother asked. "No one else in the whole world can give YOU to Jesus. Only you can give that special gift. And that makes it the best gift of all."

Please Listen, God

Please listen, God,
Please do.
I'm praying every morning;
I'm praying, God, to You.
I send my prayers
   to heaven.
Please hear me when I say,
I think of You each morning
at the start of every day.

A Very Special
Something

There is something
   very special
That I'm looking for
   today.

Until I find
   this something,
I won't go out
   to play.

I will not eat
    my breakfast.
And I will not tie
    my shoes.
Until I find
    this something,
In either
    ones or twos.

I've looked
  in every corner.
On
      the
          ceiling
and
      the
          floor.

I've looked
  inside
      my
          closet.
And, of course,
      behind
          my
              door.

But this very
　　special something
Isn't
　　in
　　　　a
　　　　　jar
　　or
　　　　jug.

'Cause this very
　　special something
Is
　　a
　　　　very
　　　　　special hug.